Tastefully Indian

Gluten Free Cookbook

Happy Cooking!

Daksha Narsing

www.spicesgourmet.com

Written by Daksha Narsing
Cover Design by Amesh Narsing
Book Design and Layout by Pravin Narsing
Photographs by Tracey Kusiewicz

ISBN 978-0-9681253-5-9

Published by:
Daksha's Gourmet Spices
107 - 1759 Sean Heights
Saanichton, B.C. Canada
V8M 0A5

www.spicesgourmet.com
e-mail: daksha@spicesgourmet.com

Printed in Canada

Cover: Jeera Salmon – page 46
Back Cover: Rotla (Millit Roti) – page 79

To

Bhaskar
Amesh
Pravin
&
Sarena

you are and always
will be
part of my universe.

Preface

The inspiration for *Tastefully Indian* came from many of my readers and customers who have gluten allergies and are looking for simple recipes that are both tasty and easy to make. Traditionally, Indian cuisine is predominantly gluten free, with the exception of a few breads, snacks and desserts. Gluten-free Indian cuisine is not only healthy but flavorful at the same time.

This cookbook, the fourth in my series, is a collection of the favorite traditional and fusion dishes I make for my own family. For the first time, I have included our family garam masala and thana jeeroo recipes. These blends, which I use in most of the recipes in this collection, will give you the wonderful flavors and aromas of Indian cooking. Daksha's Gourmet Spices will, of course, continue to package and sell our garam masala and thana jeeroo for those who don't have time to make the blends at home.

I hope the recipes in *Tastefully Indian* will introduce the uninitiated to healthy, flavorful Indian foods and increase the pleasure of those who already love to cook and eat Indian cuisine. Above all, I would like this cookbook to expand menu options for people with gluten intolerance.

Enjoy the flavors and aromas from my kitchen to yours.

Happy Cooking!

Acknowledgements

To the most important person in my life, my best friend, husband and business partner Bhaskar, thank you for your patience, understanding and loving care, which allow me to accomplish my life goals.

To my children Amesh, Pravin and Sarena, whom I look at with very proud eyes and heart, thank you for being my best critics and for providing continued love and support. Your talents and contributions have helped me to create this wonderful new cookbook.

To my editor Rhonda Bailey, thank you for making time in your busy schedule to edit *Tastefully Indian*. I'm glad you agree there is sometimes a reason that people meet each other.

Contents

Contents

Contents

Contents

Notes

Gluten Free, Indian Style

Indian cuisine is predominantly gluten free, with the exception of some breads, appetizers and desserts.

I remember in my early years, when we visited my grandmother in her village in the state of Gujarat in western India, we enjoyed amazing meals made without gluten. Many a time we had breads made from millet and curries made from a variety of vegetables, such as okra, bitter melon and beans. We enjoyed meat about once a month or on special occasions. Many varieties of fish are found in the coastal areas of the Kutch district of Gujarat, and we cooked fish once or twice a week. Our snacks or appetizers – such as Bhajyas (also known as Pakoras), Moothya, Bataka Vadas and many more – were often made with chana flour (chickpea flour).

Traditional village cooking put a lot of emphasis on maintaining a balanced diet. Vegetables and fruits were a big part of our diet. Vegetables such as okra, bitter melon and eggplant were available in abundance. Fruits such as mangoes, bananas, jackfruit and many types of berries and dates were found seasonally. Mango raas with corn rotis was one of my favorite meals.

Millet flour, corn flour, rice flour and wheat flour were the grains used for flatbreads and rotis. I always enjoyed the non-gluten rotis my grandmother made.

Spices in Indian cuisine are also gluten free. Cleaning spices took a big part of my grandmother's time. She sieved and cleaned all of her spices before grinding them with a mortar and pestle to make her blends of garam masala and thana jeeroo. This practice of cleaning spices removes any impurities. I strongly recommend that spices be cleaned and ground fresh in one's kitchen and then stored in airtight containers or packages. The alternative is to purchase ground spices from reputable companies who are known for their high quality, good, clean products.

Spices Used in this Cookbook

Seven key spices and spice blends, used in various amounts and combinations to give each dish just the right taste, are the basis of many of the recipes featured throughout *Tastefully Indian*. These spices and blends are:

1. Garam masala: an aromatic blend made with seven different spices and used in meat and lentil dishes. See page 103.
2. Thana jeeroo: a fresh-tasting blend made with coriander seeds and cumin seeds. In fact, Thana jeeroo means "coriander cumin." See page 104.
3. Whole spices: a mixture of four whole spices used to flavor the oil in some of the recipes. This mixture consists of whole cardamom, black peppercorns, cloves and cassia sticks.
4. Cumin seeds: small brown seeds used whole to flavor the oils in many vegetarian dishes.
5. Black mustard seeds: small, round black or dark brownish seeds used whole to flavor the oil.
6. Red chillie powder: finely ground dried red chillies. Chillie powder gives the dish a spicy hot taste and can be adjusted to one's heat level.
7. Turmeric powder: finely ground dried turmeric root. Turmeric powder gives food a lovely yellow color and helps with digestion.

Cooking with these spices and blends goes back many centuries. My mother and her mother before her cooked with these spices in ways that ensured each dish was satisfying, not only to the palate, but also to the body as a whole. Freshly ground spices and masalas help promote healthier bodies and reduce the incidence of colds and flus. Maintaining a balance of spices with the foods that they are used in follows the principles of Ayurveda, traditional Indian medicine.

Spice Blends

Most of the recipes in this cookbook call for freshly ground garam masala and thana jeeroo. Making these spice blends in advance will be convenient and will save you time when cooking.

Instructions to prepare your own spice blends of garam masala and thana jeeroo are on the following pages:

To make spice blends, put spices through a small sieve to remove any dust, sand, sticks, etc. Place spices on a clean stainless steel tray and sift through seeds to remove any other large impurities and leave only pure spices. Grind spice blends in a coffee grinder, and store the ground spices in glass jars in a cool dry place.

Fresh Masalas

Many of the recipes in *Tastefully Indian* call for ginger/garlic masala, green chillie masala and garlic masala. Like the ground spice blends, these fresh masalas can be made in advance to save time when cooking.

Instructions to prepare fresh masalas are found on the following pages:

These are easy to make and can be conveniently stored in the freezer.

Enjoy – and happy cooking!

Appetizers

Moothya (Spicy Patties) – page 19

Spicy Onion Rings – page 20

Spicy Chicken Wings – page 18

Pakoras – page 17

Pakoras

Ingredients:

2½ cups chana flour
5 tablespoons olive oil
3 teaspoons ginger/garlic masala
1 teaspoon green chillie masala
1 teaspoon red chillie powder
½ teaspoon turmeric powder
2 teaspoons garam masala
1 teaspoon thana jeeroo
2 teaspoons salt
1 to 2 cups water
2 cups spinach, finely chopped
2 medium onions, chopped
4 cups corn oil

Method:

1. In a large bowl, mix together chana flour, olive oil, ginger/garlic masala, green chillie masala, red chillie powder, turmeric powder, garam masala, thana jeeroo and salt.
2. Add water, a little at a time, while mixing until batter reaches the consistency of a thick paste.
3. Add chopped spinach and onions. Stir well.
4. Heat oil in wok or deep fryer on medium heat. Carefully drop about a tablespoon of pakora batter into heated oil. A small size ice-cream scoop works well.
5. Cook pakoras for about 2 to 3 minutes or until crispy golden brown. Turn occasionally.

Serve Pakoras with Tangy Tamarind Chutney. See page 91.

Spicy Chicken Wings

Ingredients:

3 to 4 pounds chicken wings
3 teaspoons ginger/garlic masala
2 teaspoons garam masala
3 teaspoons thana jeeroo
1 teaspoon red chillie powder
1 teaspoon turmeric powder
1½ teaspoons salt
3 teaspoons brown sugar
2 tablespoons olive oil
juice of ½ lemon

Method:

1. Wash and drain chicken wings.
2. In a bowl, mix together ginger/garlic masala, garam masala, thana jeeroo, red chillie powder, turmeric powder, salt, brown sugar, olive oil and juice of half a lemon.
3. Add chicken wings and toss until all the wings are coated.
4. Place on a cookie sheet and cook in 375°F oven for 45 to 50 minutes or until wings are thoroughly cooked. Turn wings over every 15 to 20 minutes.

Great appetizer!

Moothya (Spicy Patties)

Ingredients:

2 cups cooked rice
1 medium potato, grated
1 onion, finely chopped
8 tablespoons chana flour
2 teaspoons ginger/garlic masala
½ teaspoon red chillie powder
1½ teaspoons thana jeeroo
½ teaspoon turmeric powder
½ teaspoon baking powder
1½ teaspoons salt
¼ cup water (to bind mixture)
6 to 8 tablespoons corn oil (for frying)

Method:

1. In a large bowl, mix together rice, grated potato, chopped onion and chana flour.
2. Add ginger/garlic masala, red chillie powder, thana jeeroo, turmeric powder, baking powder and salt. Mix until crumbly.
3. Add just enough water to bind dough.
4. Make patties 2½ inches round and about ½ inch thick.
5. Place patties in a heated frying pan with 4 tablespoons of oil on medium heat.
6. Cook patties on one side for 2 to 3 minutes. Turn patties over and cook for a further 2 to 3 minutes or until patties are golden brown.

Spicy Onion Rings

Ingredients:

2 large onions
1¼ cups chana flour
2 tablespoons olive oil
1 teaspoon ginger/garlic masala
1 teaspoon thana jeeroo
½ teaspoon red chillie powder
1 teaspoon turmeric powder
1 teaspoon salt
1 cup water
4 cups corn oil for frying

Method:

1. Peel onions and slice into ¼-inch-thick slices. Separate the rings of onion and place in a dish. Set aside.
2. In a bowl, add chana flour, olive oil, ginger/garlic masala, thana jeeroo, red chillie powder, turmeric powder and salt.
3. Add water a little at a time and stir well until batter reaches the consistency of a pancake mix.
4. Heat oil in a wok or deep fryer on medium heat. Dip onion rings into chana flour batter and place in heated oil.
5. Cook for 3 minutes, turning rings occasionally and until onion rings are crispy golden brown.
6. Serve hot with Tangy Tamarind Chutney. See page 91.

Tastfully Indian

Chicken Tapeli

Ingredients:

2 pounds chicken breasts, cut in cubes
3 teaspoons garlic masala
½ teaspoon green chillie masala
2 teaspoons garam masala
2 teaspoons thana jeeroo
½ teaspoon red chillie powder
1 teaspoon turmeric powder
1½ teaspoons salt
6 tablespoons olive oil
2 medium onions, chopped
2 garlic cloves, thinly sliced
3 Roma tomatoes, diced
3 tablespoons cilantro, chopped

Method:

1.   Cut chicken breasts in 1-inch cubes. Wash and drain chicken.
2.   In a bowl, mix garlic masala, green chillie masala, garam masala, thana jeeroo, red chillie powder, turmeric powder and salt in 3 table-spoons olive oil to make a spice paste.
3.   Add chicken and stir well until chicken breasts are evenly coated with spices. Allow to marinate for 2 hours in the refrigerator.
4.   In a pan, heat 3 tablespoons olive oil on medium heat. Add chopped onions and thinly sliced garlic. Sauté for 3 to 5 minutes.
5.   Add marinated chicken and stir. Cook covered for 20 to 25 minutes, stirring occasionally.
6.   Add diced tomatoes and allow to cook for 5 to 10 minutes or until chicken is thoroughly cooked.
7.   Garnish with chopped cilantro.

Bataka Vadas

Step I

Ingredients:

4 potatoes, peeled and cut in chunks
2 cups water
2 teaspoons salt
2 teaspoons ginger/garlic masala
1 teaspoon green chillie masala
¼ teaspoon garam masala
1 teaspoon thana jeeroo
½ teaspoon red chillie powder
1 teaspoon turmeric powder
2 teaspoons sesame seeds
2 tablespoons cilantro, chopped
juice of one lemon

Method:

1. In a pot cook potatoes with 2 cups of water and ¼ teaspoon salt on medium heat for 25 to 30 minutes or until potatoes are thoroughly cooked.
2. Drain off any excess water and mash potatoes. Allow to cool.
3. Add ginger/garlic masala, green chillie masala, garam masala, thana jeeroo, red chillie powder, turmeric powder, sesame seeds, chopped cilantro, lemon juice and 1¾ teaspoons salt to mashed potatoes and mix all the ingredients well.
4. Make 1-inch balls and flatten them slightly to form discs. Place on a flat plate and set aside.

Bataka Vadas cont.

Step II

Ingredients:

2 cups chana flour
2 teaspoons ginger/garlic masala
1 teaspoon garam masala
1 teaspoon thana jeeroo
1 teaspoon red chillie powder
1 teaspoon turmeric powder
1¼ teaspoons salt
2 tablespoons olive oil
1¼ cups water
4 to 6 cups corn oil for frying

Method:

1. In a large bowl, mix together chana flour, ginger/garlic masala, garam masala, thana jeeroo, red chillie powder, turmeric powder, salt and olive oil.
2. Add water a little at a time while mixing continually with a whisk, until batter is a smooth consistency, like a pancake mix.
3. Heat corn oil in a wok or fryer on medium heat.
4. Dip mashed potato rounds into batter. Carefully place in hot oil in the wok and fry until crispy golden brown.

Bataka Vadas make great party snacks. Serve with Tangy Tamarind Chutney. See page 91.

Spicy Herb & Garlic Potatoes

Ingredients:

6 medium potatoes
4 tablespoons olive oil
3 garlic cloves, grated or finely chopped
2 teaspoons cumin, crushed
1 teaspoon turmeric powder
¼ teaspoon red chillie powder
2 teaspoons basil
1 teaspoon oregano
1½ teaspoons salt
2 tablespoons cilantro, chopped (optional)

Method:

1. Wash and cut peeled potatoes into half-inch cubes.
2. Heat olive oil in a large frying pan on medium heat and add potatoes.
3. Add grated or finely chopped garlic, crushed cumin, turmeric powder, red chillie powder, basil, oregano and salt. Stir well.
4. Cook covered, stirring occasionally, for about 15 to 20 minutes.
5. Remove lid and cook on low heat, turning potatoes until crispy golden brown.
6. Garnish with chopped cilantro, if desired.

Makes a great side dish or appetizer.

Papetas (Fried Eggplant)

Ingredients:

3 teaspoons ginger/garlic masala
4 teaspoons thana jeeroo
1 teaspoon cumin, crushed
1 teaspoon red chillie powder
2 teaspoons turmeric powder
1½ teaspoons salt
4 tablespoons olive oil
3 eggplants, sliced
¼ cup chana flour
½ to 1 cup corn oil for frying

Method:

1. In a bowl, mix ginger/garlic masala, thana jeeroo, crushed cumin, red chillie powder, turmeric powder, and salt with olive oil to make a spice paste.
2. Slice eggplant into ½-inch slices. Rub spice paste on both sides of eggplant slices.
3. Dip eggplant in chana flour, covering both sides.
4. In a frying pan, heat 4 tablespoons corn oil on medium heat. Place eggplant slices in pan and cook for 3 to 5 minutes each side or until eggplant is cooked.
5. Continue step 3 and 4 until all slices are cooked.

Serve with plain yogurt on the side. An excellent appetizer!

Patarya (Spicy Spinach Rolls)

Ingredients:

20 to 24 large-sized spinach leaves
1 cup chana flour
½ cup corn flour
4 tablespoons rice flour
2 tablespoons ginger/garlic masala
1 teaspoon red chillie powder
1 teaspoon turmeric powder
2 teaspoons garam masala
2 teaspoons salt
2 teaspoons sugar
juice of ½ lemon
¼ to ½ cup water
4 tablespoons oil

Method:

1. Wash and pat dry spinach leaves. Set aside.
2. In a bowl, mix together chana flour, corn flour and rice flour.
3. Add ginger/garlic masala, red chillie powder, turmeric powder, garam masala, salt, sugar, and lemon juice. Add water to make a thick paste.
4. Spread a thin layer of paste over the entire spinach leaf.
5. Take one side of leaf and fold to spine. Do the same with opposite side of leaf. Spread paste on folded parts of leaf.
6. Roll spinach leaf, just like a cabbage roll. Set aside. Follow same procedure with all the remaining spinach leaves.
7. Heat oil in a frying pan on medium heat. Place pataryas in pan and cook covered for approximately 10 to 15 minutes, turning frequently. Ensure that pataryas are evenly cooked and are crispy on the outside.

Onion Bhaji

Ingredients:

2 cups chana flour
4 tablespoons olive oil
4 teaspoons ginger/garlic masala
1 teaspoon garam masala
2 teaspoons thana jeeroo
1 teaspoon red chillie powder
1 teaspoon turmeric powder
1¾ teaspoons salt
1 cup water
2 medium onions, chopped
1½ cups green onions, chopped
½ cup cilantro, chopped
4 cups corn oil for frying

Method:

1. In a large bowl, mix together chana flour, olive oil, ginger/garlic masala, garam masala, thana jeeroo, red chillie powder, turmeric powder and salt.
2. Add water a little at a time while mixing until batter is the consistency of a thick paste.
3. Add chopped onions, chopped green onions and chopped cilantro and stir well.
4. Heat corn oil in a wok or deep fryer on medium heat. Carefully drop about a tablespoon of batter with vegetables into heated oil. A small size ice-cream scoop works well.
5. Cook, turning occasionally, for 3 minutes or until onion bhajis are crispy golden brown.

Serve with Tangy Tamarind Chutney. See page 91.

Dokra (Lentil Cake)

Ingredients for Dokra Flour Mix:

3 cups basmati rice
1½ cups chana daal
¾ cup urad daal

Ingredients:

3¾ cups dokra flour mix
2½ cups plain yogurt
3 teaspoons ginger, finely grated
½ teaspoon green chillie masala
½ teaspoon red chillie powder
½ teaspoon turmeric powder
½ teaspoon baking powder
1½ teaspoons salt
1½ cups warm water
4 tablespoons sesame seeds
4 to 6 tablespoons corn oil
2 tablespoons black mustard seeds
4 tablespoons cilantro, chopped
4 tablespoons unsweetened coconut, shredded

Method:

1. Make dokra flour mix. In a bowl, mix together basmati rice, chana daal and urad daal. Grind mixture in coffee grinder to a grainy consistency.
2. Combine in a bowl: dokra flour mix, yogurt, finely grated ginger, green chillie masala, red chillie powder, turmeric powder, baking powder and salt. Add warm water and stir well.
3. Cover and place mixture in a cool place for approximately 4 to 6 hours.

Dokra (Lentil Cake) cont.

4.   Grease 9-inch cake pans with oil.
5.   Pour mixture into cake pans, filling them half full.
6.   Sprinkle sesame seeds over top of mixture.
7.   In a large saucepan, heat enough water to cover ¼-inch depth of the saucepan. Place 2 canning jar rings in the water. Set the pan containing dokra mixture on the rings.
8.   Cover and allow dokra to cook for approximately 30 minutes on medium heat, making sure water does not evaporate completely. If needed, add more water down the side of pan, keeping water level just under the top of canning rings.
9.   To check that dokra cakes are done, poke a knife through. If the knife comes out clean, dokras are cooked.
10.   Remove dokra pan from pot and allow to cool. Place another cake pan with dokra mixture in the pot, ensuring there is enough water at the bottom of the pan at all times. Continue steam cooking dokra until mixture is used up.
11.   Cut dokra into 2-inch squares while in the pan.
12.   In a small saucepan, heat 4 tablespoons of corn oil. Add black mustard seeds. Allow seeds to pop.
13.   Drizzle small amounts of oil and black mustard seed mixture over the cut dokra.
14.   Garnish with chopped cilantro and shredded coconut.
15.   Remove dokras from pan and place them in a dish.

Makes approximately 4 to 6 pans.

Notes

Meat, Poultry & Seafood

Chicken Korma
Chicken Tikka
Butter Chicken
Indian-Style Cajun Chicken
Barbecued Garlic Chicken Kebobs
Barbecued Spicy Lamb Chops
Lamb Vindaloo
Spicy Lamb Roast
Spicy Beef Pepper Pot
Ground Beef Curry
Spicy Shepherd's Pie
Jeera Salmon
Spicy Prawns
Spicy Fried Fish

Lamb Vindaloo – page 39

Butter Chicken – page 35

Chicken Tikka – page 34

Chicken Korma – page 33

Chicken Korma

Ingredients:

3 teaspoons ginger/garlic masala
2 teaspoons garam masala
2 teaspoons thana jeeroo
1 teaspoon red chillie powder
1 teaspoon turmeric powder
1½ teaspoons salt
6 tablespoons olive oil
1½ pounds chicken breasts, cubed
2 cups of plain yogurt
2 medium onions, chopped
½ cup coconut milk
½ cup ground almonds
2 teaspoons sugar
½ cup water
2 tablespoons cilantro, chopped

Method:

1.   Mix ginger/garlic masala, garam masala, thana jeeroo, red chillie powder, turmeric powder and salt with 2 tablespoons olive oil to make a paste. Marinate cubed chicken with the paste.
2.   Add plain yogurt and stir well. Marinate for 2 to 4 hours in refrigerator.
3.   Sauté chopped onions in 4 tablespoons olive oil in a pot on medium heat. Add marinated chicken. Cover and cook for 5 to 10 minutes, stirring occasionally.
4.   Add coconut milk and ground almonds and stir well. Cook for 10 to 15 minutes. Stir occasionally.
5.   Add sugar and water. Stir. Cook for 10 to 15 minutes or until chicken is thoroughly cooked. Garnish with chopped cilantro.

Serve over a bed of basmati rice.

Chicken Tikka

Ingredients:

2 pounds chicken
3 teaspoons ginger/garlic masala
½ teaspoon green chillie masala
2 teaspoons garam masala
2 teaspoons thana jeeroo
1 teaspoon red chillie powder
1 teaspoon turmeric powder
1½ teaspoons salt
1 cup plain yogurt
juice of half a lemon
1 package wooden skewers (pre-soaked)

Method:

1. Cut chicken into 1-inch by 3-inch strips.
2. Mix ginger/garlic masala, green chillie masala, garam masala, thana jeeroo, red chillie powder, turmeric powder, salt, plain yogurt and lemon juice in a bowl. Stir well.
3. Add chicken strips and stir until chicken is well coated. Refrigerate for 3 to 6 hours.
4. Soak bamboo skewers in water for 30 minutes. (This prevents skewers from burning.) Heat barbecue on medium heat.
5. Thread marinated chicken on skewers.
6. Barbecue for 10 to 15 minutes on medium heat or until chicken is thoroughly cooked. Turn frequently.

Butter Chicken

Ingredients:

2 teaspoons ginger/garlic masala
1 teaspoon green chillie masala
1 teaspoon garam masala
1 teaspoon thana jeeroo
1 teaspoon red chillie powder
1 teaspoon turmeric powder
2 teaspoons salt
2 tablespoons olive oil
1½ pounds chicken pieces
4 tablespoons ghee or butter
½ medium onion, finely chopped

¾ cup half-and-half cream
1 cup plain yogurt
¼ cup tomato sauce (optional)
2 tablespoons cilantro, chopped

Method:

1. Mix ginger/garlic masala, green chillie masala, garam masala, thana jeeroo, red chillie powder, turmeric powder and salt with olive oil to make a spice paste.
2. Marinate chicken with spice paste for at least 2 hours in the refrigerator.
3. Heat ghee or butter in a pot and add chopped onion. Sauté until lightly browned. Add marinated chicken and stir well. Cover and cook on medium heat for 20 to 30 minutes or until chicken is thoroughly cooked.
4. Add half-and-half cream and cook for 5 to 10 minutes. Stir occasionally.
5. Add plain yogurt and stir. Cook for 5 minutes. Stir continually.
6. Add tomato sauce (optional) and cook for another 5 to 10 minutes. Stir occasionally.
7. Garnish with chopped cilantro.

   Serve over a bed of basmati rice.

Indian-Style Cajun Chicken

Ingredients:

1 pound chicken breasts (approximately 3 breasts)
1½ teaspoons ginger/garlic masala
1 teaspoon garam masala
1 teaspoon cumin, crushed
1 teaspoon paprika
½ teaspoon red chillie powder
½ teaspoon turmeric powder
½ teaspoon black pepper
½ teaspoon oregano
1 teaspoon basil
1 tablespoon lemon juice
¾ teaspoon salt
7 tablespoons olive oil
2 tablespoons cilantro, chopped

Method:

1. Slice chicken breasts horizontally in half.
2. In a large bowl, mix together ginger/garlic masala, garam masala, crushed cumin, paprika, red chillie powder, turmeric powder, black pepper, oregano, basil, lemon juice and salt with 3 tablespoons olive oil to make a paste.
3. Rub chicken breasts with paste on both sides. Marinate for 2 hours in refrigerator.
4. Heat 4 tablespoons olive oil on high heat in a pan. Sear marinated chicken breasts on both sides for 2 to 3 minutes.
5. Lower heat to medium heat and cook covered for 30 to 35 minutes or until chicken is thoroughly cooked. Turn chicken breasts occasionally.

Garnish with chopped cilantro.

Barbecued Garlic Chicken Kebobs

Ingredients:

3 teaspoons garlic masala
2 teaspoons garam masala
2 teaspoons thana jeeroo
1 teaspoon red chillie powder
1 teaspoon turmeric powder
1 tablespoon parsley, finely chopped
1 tablespoon cilantro, finely chopped
1½ teaspoons salt
3 tablespoons olive oil
2 pounds chicken
6 to 8 large garlic cloves
1 green pepper
1 red onion
1 red pepper
1 package bamboo skewers

Method:

1. Mix garlic masala, garam masala, thana jeeroo, red chillie powder, turmeric powder, finely chopped parsley, finely chopped cilantro and salt with olive oil to make a spice paste.
2. Cut chicken breasts into strips 2 to 3 inches long by 1 inch wide and about ¼ inch thick. Marinate chicken slices with spice paste.
3. Slice peeled garlic cloves into thin slices. Wrap garlic slices with marinated chicken strips.
4. Chop green pepper, red onion and red pepper into 1-inch squares.
5. Thread wrapped chicken rolls alternately with squares of green pepper, red onion and red pepper onto bamboo skewers pre-soaked in water.
6. Barbecue kebobs for 15 to 20 minutes on medium heat or until chicken is thoroughly cooked. Turn frequently.

Tastfully Indian

Barbecued Spicy Lamb Chops

Ingredients:

2 pounds lamb chops
3 teaspoons ginger/garlic masala
1 teaspoon green chillie masala
2 teaspoons garam masala
2 teaspoons thana jeeroo
1 teaspoon red chillie powder
1 teaspoon turmeric powder
½ onion, chopped finely
2 tablespoons cilantro, finely chopped
2 tablespoons parsley, finely chopped
2 teaspoons salt
3 tablespoons olive oil

Method:

1. Wash and drain lamb chops. Mix ginger/garlic masala, green chillie masala, garam masala, thana jeeroo, red chillie powder, turmeric powder, finely chopped onion, finely chopped cilantro, finely chopped parsley and salt with olive oil to make a spice paste.
2. Rub both sides of lamb chops with spice paste. Marinate lamb for 2 hours in the refrigerator.
3. Heat barbecue on medium heat. Place marinated lamb chops on grill and allow to cook for 20 to 25 minutes or until lamb is thoroughly cooked. Turn frequently.

    Serve with Cilantro Chutney. See page 92.

Lamb Vindaloo

Ingredients:

3 teaspoons ginger/garlic masala
1½ teaspoons green chillie masala
2 teaspoons garam masala
2 teaspoons thana jeeroo
2 teaspoons red chillie powder
2 teaspoon turmeric powder
1½ teaspoons salt
7 tablespoons olive oil
2 pounds lamb chops
2 medium onions, chopped
1½ cups tomato sauce
1 cup water
2 tablespoons lime juice
2 tablespoons cilantro, chopped

Method:

1. Mix ginger/garlic masala, green chillie masala, garam masala, thana jeeroo, red chillie powder, turmeric powder and salt with 3 tablespoons olive oil to make a spice paste.
2. Thoroughly blend spice paste with lamb chops and allow to marinate for 2 hours in the refrigerator.
3. Heat 4 tablespoons olive oil in a pot. Add chopped onions. Sauté.
4. Add marinated lamb and stir. Cover and cook on medium heat for 20 to 25 minutes, stirring occasionally.
5. Add tomato sauce and water. Stir. Cook for 20 to 30 minutes until curry is thick and lamb is thoroughly cooked.
6. Add lime juice and stir. Cook for 5 minutes. Garnish with chopped cilantro.

Serve over a bed of basmati rice.

Spicy Lamb Roast

Ingredients:

1 small onion, finely chopped
¼ cup parsley, finely chopped
4 teaspoons ginger/garlic masala
3 teaspoons garam masala
4 teaspoons thana jeeroo
1 teaspoon red chillie powder
2 teaspoons turmeric powder
1½ teaspoons salt
4 pounds boneless leg of lamb, butterflied
3 tablespoons olive oil
2 tablespoons chana flour
1 cup water

Method:

1. Make a spice mixture. In a large bowl, mix together chopped onions, chopped parsley, ginger/garlic masala, garam masala, thana jeeroo, red chillie powder, turmeric powder, salt and olive oil. Set 1 table-spoon of spice mixture aside.
2. Rub mixture on the inside of the butterflied leg of lamb. Roll lamb like a Swiss roll with the spice mixture inside. Tie with butcher's twine to hold lamb together.
3. Place lamb in a roasting pan on a wire rack. Rub 1 tablespoon of spice mixture on top of the lamb roast. Add ½ cup of water, just to cover the bottom of the pan. Cover and cook at 385°F oven for 1½ to 2 hours or until lamb is thoroughtly cooked. Remove lamb from pan and place on a platter. Slice lamb into desired slices.
4. Pour drippings in a saucepan. In a small bowl add chana flour and ½ cup water. Mix thoroughly until there are no lumps. Add chana flour mixture to drippings in the saucepan and cook on medium heat. Stir continuously until gravy thickens and comes to a boil. Pour gravy over lamb slices or serve on the side.

Spicy Beef Pepper Pot

Ingredients:

3 pounds beef steak, cubed
3 teaspoons ginger/garlic masala
½ teaspoon green chillie masala
2 teaspoons garam masala
4 teaspoons thana jeeroo
1 teaspoon red chillie powder
1 teaspoon turmeric powder
3 teaspoons salt
5 tablespoons olive oil
4 tablespoons chana flour
1 cup water
2 celery stalks, chopped
1 green pepper, chopped
1 red pepper, chopped
4 medium potatoes, cut in chunks
3 carrots, cut in chunks
1 red onion, cut in quarters
3 teaspoons basil
4 tablespoons cilantro, chopped

Spicy Beef Pepper Pot cont.

Method:

1.   Make spice paste to marinate beef. In a large bowl, mix together ginger/garlic masala, green chillie masala, garam masala, 2 teaspoons thana jeeroo, red chillie powder, turmeric powder and 1½ teaspoons salt with 2 tablespoons olive oil. Add beef and stir well. Marinate beef for 2 to 3 hours in the refrigerator.
2.   Heat 3 tablespoons olive oil in a frying pan on medium to high heat. Add marinated beef and stir. Cook for 5 to 10 minutes or until all the beef cubes are seared to lock in the juices.
3.   Remove beef from pan and add to a roasting pan.
4.   In a small bowl, mix together chana flour and water. Add mixture to beef in the roasting pan and stir well.
5.   Preheat oven to 400°F.
6.   In a separate large bowl, combine chopped celery, chopped green pepper, chopped red pepper, potatoes cut in chunks, carrots cut in chunks and red onion cut in quarters.
7.   Sprinkle vegetables with 1½ teaspoons salt, 2 teaspoons thana jeeroo and basil. Toss until vegetables are coated evenly with spices.
8.   Spread vegetables over beef in roasting pan. Cover and cook in oven for 50 to 60 minutes or until beef and vegetables are cooked.
9.   Garnish with chopped cilantro before serving.

Ground Beef Curry

Ingredients:

3 teaspoons ginger/garlic masala
2 teaspoons garam masala
2 teaspoons thana jeeroo
1 teaspoon red chillie powder
1½ teaspoons turmeric powder
2 teaspoons salt
5 tablespoons olive oil
1½ pounds ground beef, extra lean
2 medium onions
3 potatoes, diced
1½ cups tomato sauce
1½ cups water
2 tablespoons cilantro, chopped

Method:

1. In a bowl, mix together ginger/garlic masala, garam masala, thana jeeroo, red chillie powder, turmeric powder and salt with 2 tablespoons olive oil to make a spice paste.
2. Blend spice paste with ground beef. Marinate for 2 hours in refrigerator.
3. Grate 1 onion and add to ground beef. Blend in.
4. In a pot, heat 3 tablespoons olive oil and add 1 onion, chopped finely. Sauté. Add marinated ground beef and stir continually until beef is browned and separated. Cook for 5 to 10 minutes on medium heat.
5. Add potatoes and stir. Cook for 10 to 15 minutes.
6. Add tomato sauce and water. Stir well. Cook for 20 to 25 minutes, stirring occasionally or until beef and potatoes are cooked. Garnish with chopped cilantro.

Serve over a bed of basmati rice.

Spicy Shepherd's Pie

Step I

Ingredients:

3 teaspoons ginger/garlic masala
2 teaspoons garam masala
2 teaspoons thana jeeroo
¾ teaspoon red chillie powder
1 teaspoon turmeric powder
2½ teaspoons salt
5 tablespoons olive oil
2 pounds ground beef
2 onions, chopped
3 tablespoons chana flour
1 cup water
2 tablespoons cilantro, chopped

Method:

1. Mix ginger/garlic masala, garam masala, thana jeeroo, red chillie powder, turmeric powder and salt with 2 tablespoons olive oil to make a spice paste. Blend paste thoroughly with ground beef.
2. Heat 3 tablespoons olive oil on medium heat in a pan. Add onions and sauté.
3. Add marinated ground beef and stir continually until ground beef is browned and separated. Cook for 25 to 30 minutes or until ground beef is thoroughly cooked.
4. In a small bowl, mix chana flour and water with a whisk. Add mixture to ground beef and stir well. Cook for 5 to 10 minutes, stirring occasionally.
5. Add chopped cilantro. Stir. Remove from stove and set aside.

Spicy Shepherd's Pie cont.

Step II

Ingredients:

10 medium potatoes
4 cups water
3 tablespoons butter
1 teaspoon salt
4 tablespoons milk
1 tablespoon cilantro, chopped

Method:

1. Peel and cut potatoes into large chunks. Put potatoes into a large pot and add water, just enough to cover the potatoes. Cook for 15 to 20 minutes or until potatoes are cooked.
2. Drain off any excess water and add butter and salt. Mash potatoes and mix well. Preheat oven to 375°F.
3. Pour ground beef mixture into a 9-inch by 12-inch casserole dish. Spread ground beef evenly in the pan.
4. Top with mashed potatoes and spread evenly. Brush top of potato layer with milk.
5. Bake for 20 to 25 minutes. Broil for 3 to 5 minutes or until potato topping is golden brown.
6. Garnish with chopped cilantro before serving.

Serve hot.

Jeera Salmon

Ingredients:

2 pounds salmon fillet
½ onion, finely chopped
3 tablespoons green onions, finely chopped
3 tablespoons cilantro, finely chopped
3 teaspoons garlic masala
2 teaspoons thana jeeroo
3 teaspoons cumin, crushed
½ teaspoon red chillie powder
1 teaspoon turmeric powder
1 teaspoon salt
5 tablespoons olive oil
1 teaspoon cumin seeds
3 tablespoons butter

Method:

1. Cut salmon fillet into 1-inch by 3-inch strips.
2. Combine onion, green onions, 2 tablespoons finely chopped cilantro, garlic masala, thana jeeroo, crushed cumin, red chillie powder, turmeric powder and salt with 3 tablespoons of olive oil to make a spice paste.
3. Coat salmon strips with spice paste and marinate for 2 hours in the refrigerator.
4. Heat 2 tablespoons olive oil in a frying pan and add cumin seeds.
5. Place salmon gently in the pan and cover and cook for 5 to 10 minutes on medium heat.
6. Turn salmon once only and cook on low heat for 15 to 20 minutes or until salmon is cooked.
7. Spread butter over salmon and allow butter to melt. Garnish with 1 tablespoon chopped cilantro and serve.

Spicy Prawns

Ingredients:

2 pounds fresh prawns peeled
5 tablespoons olive oil
4 teaspoons garlic masala
3 teaspoons thana jeeroo
3 teaspoons cumin, crushed
1 teaspoon red chillie powder
1 teaspoon turmeric powder
1½ teaspoons salt
1 teaspoon cumin seeds
1 bunch green onions, chopped
2 medium onions, chopped
6 Roma tomatoes, diced

3 tablespoons butter
juice of half a lemon
2 tablespoons cilantro, chopped

Method:

1. Make a spice mixture to coat prawns. In a bowl, mix together, 2 tablespoons olive oil, 1 teaspoon garlic masala, 1 teaspoon thana jeeroo, 2 teaspoons crushed cumin, ½ teaspoon red chillie powder, ½ teaspoon turmeric powder and ½ teaspoon salt. Add prawns and toss to coat all the prawns.
2. In a pan heat 3 tablespoons olive oil on medium heat. Add cumin seeds, chopped onions and green onions. Sauté.
3. Add diced tomatoes, 3 teaspoons garlic masala, 2 teaspoons thana jeeroo, 1 teaspoon crushed cumin, ½ teaspoon red chillie powder, ½ teaspoon turmeric powder and 1 teaspoon salt. Cook for 10 to 15 minutes stirring occasionally. Add marinated prawns to onion and tomato sauce and cook prawns for 2 minutes, stirring continuously. Remove from heat.
4. Add butter and stir until butter has melted. Squeeze juice of half a lemon over spicy prawns and garnish with chopped cilantro. Serve over a bed of basmati rice.

Spicy Fried Fish

Ingredients:

2 teaspoons garlic masala
½ teaspoon green chillie masala
2 teaspoons cumin, crushed
2 teaspoon thana jeeroo
½ teaspoon red chillie powder
1 teaspoon turmeric powder
1 teaspoon salt
5 tablespoons olive oil
1½ pounds fish steaks (cod, halibut, salmon, snapper or sole)
¼ cup chana flour
2 tablespoons cilantro, chopped
1 lemon, cut in wedges

Method:

1. Combine garlic masala, green chillie masala, crushed cumin, thana jeeroo, red chillie powder, turmeric powder and salt with 2 tablespoons olive oil to make a spice paste.
2. Coat fish steaks with spice paste on both sides and marinate for 2 hours in the refrigerator.
3. Coat fish lightly with chana flour. Heat 3 tablespoons olive oil in a frying pan on medium heat.
4. Add marinated fish steaks and cook for 10 to 15 minutes. Turn fish occasionally until cooked and golden brown.
5. Garnish with chopped cilantro and lemon wedges.

Aloo Gobi – page 58

Green Bean Curry – page 56

Vegetarian Dishes

Paneer
Muttar Paneer
Chana Masala
Spinach Curry
Spicy Potatoes
Green Bean Curry
Vegetable Korma
Aloo Gobi
Raveya (Stuffed Eggplant)
Okra Curry
Bitter Melon Curry

Paneer

Ingredients:

5 cups homogenized milk
juice of ½ lemon

Method:

1. In a large pot, heat milk to a rolling boil.
2. Add lemon juice slowly, stirring constantly. Milk will separate.
3. Remove pot from stove and continue stirring until milk is completely separated.
4. Cool mixture for 5 to 10 minutes. Strain mixture through 4 layers of cheesecloth or a clean cotton cloth. Gather edges of cloth and squeeze slightly to drain off any excess whey.
5. Place cloth on a cutting board and shape cheese into a rectangle of about ½ inch thick on the cloth. Fold flaps of cloth over cheese to cover completely.
6. Wrap again in more cheesecloth or kitchen towels and place on a cookie sheet. Place a cutting board or another cookie sheet on top. Put weights on board to squeeze out any excess whey left in cheese.
7. Allow cheese to sit with weights on top for 1 to 4 hours. Remove weights and unfold cloth.
8. Place cheese on a cutting board and cut into 1-inch squares. Store in a sealed container in the refrigerator.
9. Paneer is ready to use.

Muttar Paneer

Ingredients:

2 tablespoons olive oil
1 teaspoon cumin seeds
1 cup paneer, cubed (see page 51)
1 medium onion, chopped
3 medium potatoes, diced
3 teaspoons ginger/garlic masala
½ teaspoon green chillie masala
2 teaspoons thana jeeroo
½ teaspoon garam masala
½ teaspoon red chillie powder
1 teaspoon turmeric powder
1½ teaspoons salt
2½ cups water
2 cups frozen peas
4 Roma tomatoes, diced
1 cup tomato sauce
1 tablespoon cilantro, chopped

Method:

1. Heat olive oil in a pan on medium heat. Add cumin seeds and paneer. Sauté until paneer is golden brown. Remove from pan and set aside.
2. Add chopped onion and sauté.
3. Add diced potatoes, ginger/garlic masala, green chillie masala, thana jeeroo, garam masala, red chillie powder, turmeric powder, salt and ½ cup water. Stir well.
4. Cover and allow to cook for 10 to 15 minutes or until potatoes are cooked. Stir occasionally.
5. Add peas, sautéed paneer, diced tomatoes, tomato sauce and 2 cups water. Cook for 10 to 15 minutes. Stir occasionally.
6. Garnish with chopped cilantro.

Chana Masala

Ingredients:

3 tablespoons olive oil
1 teaspoon cumin seeds
½ onion, chopped
2 cups chickpeas, cooked
½ green pepper, diced
2 teaspoons ginger/garlic masala
2 teaspoons thana jeeroo
½ teaspoon garam masala
1 teaspoon red chillie powder
1 teaspoon turmeric powder
1½ teaspoons salt
1 cup tomato sauce
1 tablespoon brown sugar
2 tablespoons cilantro, chopped

Method:

1. Heat olive oil in a pan on medium heat and add cumin seeds. Allow seeds to sizzle.
2. Add chopped onions and sauté.
3. Add chickpeas, green pepper, ginger/garlic masala, thana jeeroo, garam masala, red chillie powder, turmeric powder and salt. Stir.
4. Cook for 10 to 15 minutes, stirring occasionally.
5. Add tomato sauce and brown sugar. Stir.
6. Cook on low heat, stirring occasionally, for 5 to 10 minutes or until chickpeas are thoroughly cooked.
7. Garnish with chopped cilantro.

Spinach Curry

Ingredients:

4 tablespoons olive oil
2 teaspoons cumin seeds
1 medium onion, chopped
2 potatoes, cut in chunks
2 teaspoons ginger/garlic masala
½ teaspoon green chillie masala
2 teaspoons thana jeeroo
½ teaspoon red chillie powder
1 teaspoon turmeric powder
1½ teaspoons salt
8 cups spinach, chopped
2 tomatoes, diced

Method:

1.	Heat olive oil in a pan on medium heat. Add cumin seeds. Allow seeds to brown. Add chopped onion and sauté.
2.	Add potatoes, ginger/garlic masala, green chillie masala, thana jeeroo, red chillie powder, turmeric powder and salt. Stir well. Cook covered for 5 to 10 minutes.
3.	Add chopped spinach and cook for 15 to 20 minutes, stirring occasionally.
4.	Add diced tomatoes. Cook for 10 to 15 minutes on low heat. Stir occasionally.

Serve with Rotla (Millet Roti–see page 79) and plain yogurt.

Spicy Potatoes

Ingredients:

6 tablespoons olive oil
1 teaspoon cumin seeds
1 teaspoon black mustard seeds
4 potatoes, thinly sliced
2 teaspoons ginger/garlic masala
½ teaspoon green chillie masala
1 teaspoon thana jeeroo
½ teaspoon red chillie powder
1 teaspoon turmeric powder
1½ teaspoons salt
2 tablespoons cilantro, chopped

Method:

1. Heat olive oil in a frying pan on medium heat. Add cumin seed and black mustard seeds. Allow seeds to brown and pop.
2. Add sliced potatoes, ginger/garlic masala, green chillie masala, thana jeeroo, red chillie powder, turmeric powder and salt. Stir well.
3. Cover and cook for 15 to 20 minutes. Stir occasionally or until potatoes are cooked and golden brown.
4. Garnish with chopped cilantro.

Green Bean Curry

Ingredients:

3 tablespoons olive oil
3 teaspoons cumin seeds
2 medium onions, chopped
6 cups green beans, chopped
4 potatoes, diced
3 teaspoons ginger/garlic masala
3 teaspoons thana jeeroo
½ teaspoon red chillie powder
1 teaspoon turmeric powder
2 teaspoons salt
½ cup water
4 Roma tomatoes, diced
2 tablespoons cilantro, chopped

Method:

1. Heat olive oil in a pan on medium heat. Add cumin seeds.
2. Add chopped onions. Sauté until onions are slightly browned.
3. Add chopped green beans, potatoes, ginger/garlic masala, thana jeeroo, red chillie powder, turmeric powder, salt and water. Stir well.
4. Cook for 20 to 25 minutes, stirring occasionally.
5. Add tomatoes and stir. Allow to cook for 15 to 20 minutes or until potatoes and green beans are cooked.
6. Garnish with chopped cilantro.

Vegetable Korma

Ingredients:

2 tablespoons olive oil
2 teaspoons cumin seeds
1 onion, chopped
¼ cup slivered almonds
3 cups cauliflower, cut in chunks
2 potatoes, cut in chunks
3 carrots, chopped
3 teaspoons ginger/garlic masala
3 teaspoons thana jeeroo
1 teaspoon red chillie powder
1 teaspoon turmeric powder
2½ teaspoons salt
1 cup water
1 cup coconut milk
3 teaspoons brown sugar

juice of one lemon
2 tablespoons cilantro, chopped

Method:

1. Heat olive oil in a pot on medium heat. Add cumin seeds and chopped onion. Sauté.
2. Add slivered almonds and cook until almonds are slightly browned.
3. Add cauliflower, potatoes and carrots. Stir.
4. Add ginger/garlic masala, thana jeeroo, red chillie powder, turmeric powder, salt and water. Cook for 10 to 15 minutes, stirring occasionally.
5. Add coconut milk and brown sugar. Stir well.
6. Cook for 5 minutes stirring occasionally. Add juice of 1 lemon and cook for 5 minutes.
7. Garnish with chopped cilantro.

Aloo Gobi

Ingredients:

4 tablespoons olive oil
1 teaspoon cumin seeds
1 onion, chopped
2 cups cauliflower, chopped
2 potatoes, diced
2 teaspoons ginger/garlic masala
½ teaspoon green chillie masala
2 teaspoons thana jeeroo
1 teaspoon red chillie powder
1 teaspoon turmeric powder
1½ teaspoons salt
1 cup frozen peas
2 tomatoes, diced
2 tablespoons cilantro, chopped

Method:

1. Heat olive oil in a pan on medium heat. Add cumin seeds. Add chopped onion. Sauté.
2. Add cauliflower, potatoes, ginger/garlic masala, green chillie masala, thana jeeroo, red chillie powder, turmeric powder and salt. Stir well.
3. Cover and cook for 10 minutes, stirring occasionally.
4. Add frozen peas and cook for 5 minutes.
5. Add tomatoes and cook on low heat for 5 to 10 minutes, stirring occasionally. Garnish with chopped cilantro.

Serve with Corn Roti. See page 81.

Raveya (Stuffed Eggplant)

Ingredients:

6 eggplants, small to medium size
1 medium onion, chopped finely
3 tablespoons unsalted peanuts, crushed
2 teaspoons ginger/garlic masala
½ teaspoon green chillie masala
2 teaspoons thana jeeroo
½ teaspoon red chillie powder
1 teaspoon turmeric powder
2 tablespoons cilantro, chopped
1½ teaspoons salt
4 tablespoons olive oil

Method:

1.   Wash eggplants and cut tops off. Scoop out centre of each eggplant and place the scooped-out eggplant in a bowl. Set aside.
2.   In another bowl, mix together chopped onion, crushed peanuts, ginger/garlic masala, green chillie masala, thana jeeroo, red chillie powder, turmeric powder, chopped cilantro, salt and olive oil to make a stuffing.
3.   Chop scooped-out eggplant into small pieces and add to onion and spice stuffing.
4.   Fill each eggplant with stuffing as tightly as possible.
5.   In a large pot, heat olive oil on low heat and gently place stuffed eggplants in the pot. Cover and cook for 25 to 30 minutes or until eggplants are thoroughly cooked. Turn frequently.

Okra Curry

Ingredients:

4 tablespoons olive oil
1 teaspoon cumin seeds
1 onion, chopped
2 cups okra, thinly sliced
1½ teaspoons ginger/garlic masala
½ teaspoon green chillie masala
2 teaspoons thana jeeroo
½ teaspoon red chillie powder
1 teaspoon turmeric powder
1½ teaspoons salt
2 tomatoes, diced
2 tablespoons cilantro, chopped

Method:

1.   Heat oil in a pan on medium heat. Add cumin seeds. Add chopped onion. Sauté.
2.   Add okra, ginger/garlic masala, green chillie masala, thana jeeroo, red chillie powder, turmeric powder and salt. Stir well.
3.   Cover and cook for 10 to 15 minutes. Stir occasionally.
4.   Add tomatoes and cook for 10 to 15 minutes or until okra is cooked and browned.
5.   Garnish with chopped cilantro.

Serve with Rotla (Millet Roti). See page 79.

Bitter Melon Curry

Ingredients:

2 cups bitter melon, thinly sliced
3 teaspoons salt
2 cups water
4 tablespoons olive oil
2 teaspoons cumin seeds
1 onion, chopped
2 teaspoons ginger/garlic masala
½ teaspoon green chillie masala
2 teaspoons thana jeeroo
½ teaspoon red chillie powder
1 teaspoon turmeric powder
2 tomatoes, chopped
2 tablespoons cilantro, chopped

Method:

1.   In a large bowl, place thinly sliced bitter melon in a brine made by dissolving 2 teaspoons salt in 2 cups of water. Soak for 30 minutes.
2.   Drain and rinse bitter melon. Set aside.
3.   Heat olive oil in a frying pan on medium heat and add cumin seeds.
4.   Add chopped onion and sauté. Add bitter melon. Stir.
5.   Add ginger/garlic masala, green chillie masala, thana jeeroo, red chillie powder, turmeric powder and 1 teaspoon salt.
6.   Cook for 10 to 15 minutes stirring occasionally.
7.   Add tomatoes and cook for 10 to 15 minutes. Stir occasionally.
8.   Garnish with chopped cilantro.

Notes

Daals, Lentils & Soups

Sprouted Mung Bean Curry
Mixed Lentil Daal
Red Lentils with Green Beans
Mung Bean Onion Curry
Zucchini with Chana Daal
Spicy Black-Eyed Beans
Dadima's Onion Soup
Vegetable Lentil Soup
Spicy Chicken Soup
Bhakro

Mixed Lentil Daal – page 66

Mung Bean Onion Curry – page 68

Sprouted Mung Bean Curry

Ingredients:

1 cup mung beans
3½ cups warm water
4 tablespoons olive oil
1½ onions, thinly sliced
1 teaspoon ginger/garlic masala
¼ teaspoon green chillie masala
1 teaspoon thana jeeroo
½ teaspoon red chillie powder
1 teaspoon turmeric powder
1 teaspoon salt

Method:

1. Soak mung beans in 3 cups of warm water in a large bowl. Soak for approximately 3 hours or until beans expand to twice their size.
2. Drain and tie beans in a clean cheesecloth or kitchen towel. Place bundle of beans in a deep dish. Store in a dark place for 10 to 12 hours or until beans have sprouted.
3. Remove sprouted beans from cloth. Wash beans gently, trying not to break the sprouts. Drain off excess water.
4. In a large saucepan, heat olive oil on medium heat. Add onions and sauté.
5. Add sprouted beans, ginger/garlic masala, green chillie masala, thana jeeroo, red chillie powder, turmeric powder, ½ cup water and salt. Stir.
6. Cook in a covered pot on low heat for approximately 40 to 60 minutes, or until beans are thoroughly cooked. Stir occasionally.

Mixed Lentil Daal

Ingredients:

½ cup mung daal
½ cup urad daal
½ cup red lentils
2 tablespoons olive oil
3 teaspoons ginger/garlic masala
1½ teaspoons garam masala
½ teaspoon thana jeeroo
½ teaspoon red chillie powder
1 teaspoon turmeric powder
1½ teaspoons salt
8 cups water

Method:

1. In a bowl, mix mung daal, urad daal and red lentils. Wash these mixed lentils with warm water. Drain off water.
2. In a pot, heat olive oil on medium heat. Add ginger/garlic masala and sauté.
3. Add washed mixed lentils and stir.
4. Add 1 teaspoon garam masala, thana jeeroo, red chillie powder, turmeric powder and salt. Stir.
5. Add water and cook covered for 30 to 35 minutes stirring occasionally or until daal is cooked.
6. Garnish with ½ teaspoon garam masala.

Serve with Corn Roti. See page 81.

Red Lentils with Green Beans

Ingredients:

2 cups red lentils
1 tablespoon olive oil
1 teaspoon ginger/garlic masala
1 teaspoon garam masala
½ teaspoon thana jeeroo
½ teaspoon red chillie powder
½ teaspoon turmeric powder
1 teaspoon salt
5 cups water
2 cups green bean curry. See page 56.
1 tablespoon chopped cilantro

Method:

1.	Wash red lentils with warm water. Drain water and set aside.
2.	In a pot, heat olive oil on medium heat and add ginger/garlic masala, red lentils, garam masala, thana jeeroo, red chillie powder, turmeric powder and salt. Stir well.
3.	Add 4 cups water and stir. Cook covered for 10 to 15 minutes, stirring occasionally.
4.	Add green bean curry and 1 cup water and stir. Cook for 5 to 10 minutes or until lentils are cooked.
5.	Garnish with chopped cilantro.

Serve with Corn Roti. See page 81.

Mung Bean Onion Curry

Ingredients:

1 cup mung beans
4 cups water
3 tablespoons olive oil
1 onion, finely chopped
1 tomato, diced
1½ teaspoons ginger/garlic masala
½ teaspoon garam masala
1 teaspoon thana jeeroo
½ teaspoon red chillie powder
1 teaspoon turmeric powder
1 teaspoon salt
1 tablespoon cilantro, chopped

Method:

1. Wash mung beans. Cook on medium heat in a pan with 3 cups water for 30 to 40 minutes or until mung beans are thoroughly cooked. Set aside.
2. Heat olive oil in a pan and add finely chopped onion. Sauté.
3. Add tomato, ginger/garlic masala, garam masala, thana jeeroo, red chillie powder, turmeric powder and salt. Stir.
4. Cook for 10 to 15 minutes, stirring occasionally.
5. Add cooked mung beans and 1 cup of water. Stir and cook for 15 to 20 minutes.
6. Garnish with chopped cilantro.

Serve with plain yogurt and Rotla (Millet Roti). See page79.

Zucchini with Chana Daal

Ingredients:

1 cup chana daal
3½ cups warm water
1 teaspoon ginger/garlic masala
¼ teaspoon green chillie masala
½ teaspoon red chillie powder
1 teaspoon turmeric powder
½ teaspoon salt
3 tablespoons olive oil
½ teaspoon black mustard seeds
1 small zucchini, cut in chunks
2 tablespoons cilantro, chopped

Method:

1. Soak chana daal in 3 cups warm water for about 3 hours or until daal expands to twice its original size.
2. Wash chana daal and drain off excess water. Add ginger/garlic masala, green chillie masala, red chillie powder, turmeric powder and salt. Stir well.
3. Heat olive oil in a pan on medium heat. Add black mustard seeds and allow seeds to pop in the hot oil.
4. Add chana daal and stir. Add ½ cup water. Cook covered on medium heat for 10 to 15 minutes or until daal is half cooked.
5. Add zucchini. Stir. Cover and allow to cook on low heat for another 10 to 15 minutes or until both daal and zucchini are cooked.
6. Garnish with chopped cilantro.

Spicy Black-Eyed Beans

Ingredients:

1 cup black-eyed beans
4½ cups water
1 teaspoon ginger/garlic masala
1 teaspoon thana jeeroo
½ teaspoon red chillie powder
¼ teaspoon turmeric powder
1 teaspoon salt
4 tablespoons olive oil
10 to 12 ajwain seeds
½ onion, chopped
1 tomato, diced
½ cup tomato sauce
2 teaspoons white wine vinegar
1 teaspoon sweet basil
½ teaspoon oregano
1 tablespoon brown sugar

Method:

1. Cook beans in 4 cups of water on medium heat for 20 to 30 minutes or until beans are fully cooked.
2. Drain beans and place in a deep dish. Add ginger/garlic masala, thana jeeroo, red chillie powder, turmeric powder and salt.
3. Heat olive oil in a saucepan on medium heat. Add ajwain seeds and chopped onion. Sauté.
4. Add beans and stir. Add diced tomato, tomato sauce, ½ cup water, vinegar, sweet basil and oregano. Stir well.
5. Add brown sugar and stir. Cook for 20 to 30 minutes on low heat.

Serve with plain yogurt.

Dadima's Onion Soup

Step I

Ingredients:

2 tablespoons olive oil
7 small onions, diced
2 teaspoons ginger, grated
¼ teaspoon red chillie powder
½ teaspoon turmeric powder
1½ teaspoons salt
6 cups water
juice of half a lemon

Method:

1.   In a saucepan, heat olive oil on medium heat and add onions. Cook for 3 to 5 minutes, stirring frequently.
2.   Add grated ginger, red chillie powder, turmeric powder, salt and water. Stir well and cook for 30 to 40 minutes, stirring occasionally.
3.   Set aside and allow to cool down.
4.   Pour onion mixture into a blender and blend to a smooth consistency.
5.   Add juice of half a lemon. Stir. Set aside.

Continued on next page.

Dadima's Onion Soup cont.

Step II

Ingredients:

1½ tablespoons olive oil
pinch of crushed chillies
1 teaspoon cumin seeds
1 teaspoon black mustard seeds
onion soup mixture from Step I
1 cup water
2 tablespoons brown sugar
1 tablespoon cilantro, chopped

Method:

1. In a pot, heat olive oil on medium heat.
2. Add crushed red chillies, cumin seeds and black mustard seeds. Allow seeds to pop.
3. Add onion soup mixture and cover quickly to trap in flavors for a minute.
4. Add water and brown sugar. Cook for 5 to 10 minutes. Bring to a rolling boil and stir frequently.
5. Garnish with chopped cilantro.

Serve over a bed of basmati rice.

Vegetable Lentil Soup

Ingredients:

1 cup mung daal
1 cup red lentils
2 tablespoons olive oil
1 onion, chopped
1 potato, diced
1 cup celery, chopped
3 carrots, chopped
3 teaspoons ginger/garlic masala
1 teaspoon garam masala
3 teaspoons thana jeeroo
1 teaspoon red chillie powder
1 teaspoon turmeric powder
2 teaspoons salt
8 cups water
2 tablespoons cilantro, chopped

Method:

1. Wash and drain mung daal and red lentils together in a dish. Set aside.
2. Heat olive oil in a pot on medium heat. Add chopped onion and sauté.
3. Add diced potato, chopped celery and chopped carrots. Stir.
4. Add ginger/garlic masala, garam masala, thana jeeroo, red chillie powder, turmeric powder, salt and washed lentils. Stir well.
5. Add water and cook, stirring occasionally, for 35 to 40 minutes or until vegetables and lentils are cooked.
6. Garnish with chopped cilantro.

Spicy Chicken Soup

Ingredients:

2 boneless, skinless chicken breasts
4 medium carrots, diced
2 cups celery, chopped
3 potatoes, diced
1 cup leeks, chopped
1 small rutabaga, diced
1 small parsnip, diced
1 onion, chopped
¼ teaspoon garam masala
½ teaspoon thana jeeroo
¼ teaspoon ground black pepper
¼ teaspoon red chillie powder
½ teaspoon turmeric powder
3 teaspoons salt
10 cups water
3 tablespoons butter

¼ cup chana flour
1 tablespoon cilantro, chopped
1 tablespoon parsley, chopped

Method:

1. In a large pot, combine chicken breasts, carrots, celery, potatoes, leek, rutabaga, parsnip, onion, garam masala, thana jeeroo, ground black pepper, red chillie powder, turmeric powder, salt, 8 cups water and butter.

2. Cook on medium heat for 20 minutes. Remove chicken breasts and cut into ½-inch cubes. Add cubed chicken back into the soup. Continue cooking for another 30 minutes.

3. Mix chana flour in 2 cups of water and add to soup. Cook for 20 to 25 minutes, stirring occasionally or until vegetables and chicken are cooked. Garnish with chopped parsley and cilantro.

Bhakro

Ingredients:

3¾ cup dokra flour. See page 28.
2½ cups plain yogurt
1 cup warm water
2 teaspoons ginger/garlic masala
1 teaspoon green chillie masala
½ teaspoon red chillie powder
1 teaspoon turmeric powder
1 teaspoon baking powder
2 teaspoons salt
1 medium onion, sliced
2 cups spinach, finely chopped
4 tablespoons sesame seeds
6 tablespoons corn oil
1 tablespoon black mustard seeds
2 tablespoons cilantro, chopped

Method:

1. In a bowl, combine dokra flour, plain yogurt, warm water, ginger/garlic masala, green chillie masala, red chillie powder, turmeric powder, baking powder and salt. Stir and cover. Let mixture sit for 2 to 4 hours.
2. Add sliced onion and chopped spinach. Stir.
3. Grease a 9-inch by 13-inch baking dish and pour mixture in. Spread evenly and sprinkle with sesame seeds
4. Bake in a preheated oven at 375°F for 40 to 45 minutes. Remove pan from oven and cut bhakro into 2-inch squares. Set aside.
5. In a small saucepan heat corn oil and add black mustard seeds. Allow seeds to pop. Pour oil with black mustard seeds evenly over bhakro.
6. Garnish with chopped cilantro. Remove bhakro from pan and place on a platter.

Notes

Flatbreads & Rice

Rotla (Millet Roti)
Spicy Rice Puri
Corn Roti
Poora (Spicy Crepes)
Rice with Red Lentils
Basmati Rice
Spicy Lemon Rice
Yellow Rice with Onions
Vegetable Pilaf
Ghee (Clarified Butter)

Rotla (Millet Roti)

Ingredients:

4 cups millet flour
½ teaspoon salt
1 tablespoon olive oil
2 cups water

Method:

1. In a bowl, combine millet flour, salt and olive oil. Bind dough with water.
2. Make dough into balls 1 to 2 inches round.
3. Grease a thin, food-safe plastic mat with olive oil. (A food-safe freezer bag works well.)
4. Place each ball of dough on one half of plastic mat and fold other half of mat over dough.
5. Using a rolling pin, roll dough into a 4-inch to 5-inch round.
6. Heat tawa or non-stick pan on medium heat. Cook rotla lightly on one side for 15 seconds.
7. Turn rotla over and cook for 20 to 30 seconds or until light brown.
8. Turn rotla again and cook until rotla puffs up or is light brown on both sides.
9. Remove from pan and pile rotla on a flat plate. Spread ghee or butter on hot rotlas.

Serve hot Rotla with many of the dishes in this cookbook.

Spicy Rice Puri

Ingredients:

1 cup rice flour
½ cup water
¼ teaspoon ginger/garlic masala
¼ teaspoon red chillie powder
¼ teaspoon turmeric powder
1 tablespoon cilantro, chopped
½ teaspoon salt
1 tablespoon olive oil
2 to 3 cups corn oil for frying

Method:

1. In a saucepan, mix ½ cup rice flour and water until smooth. Add ginger/garlic masala, red chillie powder, turmeric powder, chopped cilantro, salt and olive oil. Stir well.
2. Cook on medium heat for 2 to 3 minutes stirring constantly or until dough starts to thicken and form lumps. Remove from stove.
3. Add rest of the rice flour immediately and stir until a soft dough is formed. Knead dough.
4. Heat corn oil on medium to high heat in a wok or fryer.
5. Grease hands and make 1-inch balls of dough. Pat dough between both palms to form a 2-inch, flat puri.
6. Carefully place puri in the hot corn oil and fry for 2 to 3 minutes or until puris are crispy golden brown.

Rotla (Millet Roti) – page 79

Spicy Lemon Rice – page 85

Corn Roti

Ingredients:

2 cups corn flour
1 cup water
1 teaspoon salt
2 tablespoons olive oil

Method:

1. In a saucepan, mix 1 cup corn flour and water until smooth. Add salt and olive oil. Stir well.
2. Cook on medium heat, stirring constantly, for 2 to 3 minutes or until dough starts to thicken and form lumps. Add rest of the corn flour immediately and stir until a soft dough is formed. Remove from stove.
3. Knead dough and form into 1-inch balls.
4. Grease a thin, food-safe plastic mat with olive oil. (A food-safe freezer bag works well). Place each ball of dough on one half of plastic mat and fold other half of mat over dough.
5. Use a rolling pin to roll dough into 4- to 5-inch rounds.
6. Heat tawa or non-stick pan on medium heat. Cook roti lightly on one side for 15 seconds.
7. Turn roti over and cook for 20 to 30 seconds or until light brown.
8. Turn roti again and cook until roti puffs up or is light brown on both sides.
9. Remove from pan and pile roti on a flat plate. Spread ghee or butter on hot rotis.

Serve Corn Roti with many of the dishes in this cookbook.

Poora (Spicy Crepes)

Ingredients:

½ cup chana flour
2 cups rice flour
½ teaspoon turmeric powder
1 teaspoon green chillie masala
2 tablespoons cilantro, finely chopped
2 teaspoons salt
3 cups water
¼ cup corn oil

Method:

1. In a large bowl, mix together chana flour, rice flour, turmeric powder, green chillie masala, finely chopped cilantro, salt and water. Cover and let mixture sit for an hour in a cool place.
2. Heat tawa or non-stick pan on medium heat. Brush oil on tawa or pan. Pour mixture, using a ladle, around the edge of the tawa.
3. Spread mixture evenly in a thin layer on the surface of the tawa.
4. Cook poora on one side until golden brown.
5. Flip poora over. Brush oil around the outside edge of the poora and cook until golden brown. Remove and pile on a flat plate.
6. Continue steps 2 to 5 until mixture is used up.

Serve with curries or enjoy as a snack.

Rice with Red Lentils

Ingredients:

2 cups rice
3 tablespoons butter
2 teaspoons whole cumin seeds
3 cups water
1 teaspoon salt
½ cup red lentils

Method:

1. Wash rice and set aside. Melt butter in a saucepan on medium heat and add cumin seeds.
2. Add washed rice and stir.
3. Add water and salt. Stir well.
4. Cook for 10 to 15 minutes on medium heat.
5. Add red lentils and stir.
6. Cook for a further 15 to 20 minutes on low heat or until rice and lentils are cooked.

Basmati Rice

Ingredients:

1 cup basmati rice
4½ cups water
1 teaspoon salt
1 tablespoon ghee or butter

Method:

1. Wash* basmati rice 3 times in warm water until water is clear. Put washed rice in a large pot.
2. Cook rice on medium heat with approximately 4 cups of water.
3. Add salt and stir. Cook for 10 to 15 minutes or until rice is half cooked.
4. Drain rice in a colander. Set aside.
5. Coat bottom of the pot with ½ tablespoon ghee or butter. Add drained rice. Spread ½ tablespoon ghee or butter on top of rice.
6. Add ½ cup of water. Cover and cook for 10 to 15 minutes on low heat or until rice is fully cooked.

* Basmati rice is a thin, long grain rice. These grains should be washed 3 times in a bowl with warm water. The first wash will leave milky water, which is drained off. After the third washing, the water should be clear. This indicates the rice is clear of any white starch and therefore will not stick together when cooked.

Spicy Lemon Rice

Ingredients:

3 tablespoons olive oil
2 teaspoons cumin seeds
1 teaspoon black mustard seeds
2 onions, chopped
4 potatoes, diced
3 cups cooked rice
3 teaspoons ginger/garlic masala
2 teaspoons thana jeeroo
½ teaspoon red chillie powder
1 teaspoon turmeric powder
2 teaspoons salt
1 cup water
Juice of half a lemon
3 tablespoons cilantro, chopped
2 tablespoons sesame seeds

Method:

1. Heat olive oil in a pan on medium heat. Add cumin seeds, black mustard seeds and onions. Sauté.
2. Add potatoes. Stir and cook, covered, for 3 to 5 minutes.
3. Add cooked rice, ginger/garlic masala, thana jeeroo, red chillie powder, turmeric powder, salt and water. Stir well and cook for 5 to 10 minutes.
4. Add lemon juice and cook for 5 to 10 minutes, stirring occasionally.
5. Garnish with chopped cilantro and sesame seeds.

Yellow Rice with Onions

Ingredients:

2 cups basmati rice
3 tablespoons ghee or butter
1 teaspoon cumin seeds
½ onion, finely sliced
1 teaspoon salt
½ teaspoon turmeric powder
4 cups water

Method:

1. Wash rice 3 times in warm water until water is clear. Drain water and set aside.
2. Heat butter in a saucepan on medium heat. Add cumin seeds and onion and sauté.
3. Add rice, salt, turmeric powder and water. Stir.
4. Cook rice on medium heat for 15 to 20 minutes or until rice is cooked.

Vegetable Pilaf

Ingredients:

2 cups basmati rice
2½ cups water
3½ teaspoons salt
4 tablespoons olive oil
2 teaspoons cumin seeds
1 onion, chopped
2 medium potatoes, diced
2 carrots, chopped
2 cups frozen peas
2 teaspoons ginger/garlic masala
½ teaspoon green chillie masala
2 teaspoons thana jeeroo
½ teaspoon red chillie powder

1 teaspoon turmeric powder
1 tablespoon cilantro, chopped
1 tablespoon sesame seeds

Method:

1. Wash basmati rice 3 times and cook in a pan with 2 cups of water and 2 teaspoons salt. Cook rice on medium heat for 10 to 15 minutes or until rice is half cooked. Remove from stove and drain off water in a sieve and set aside.

2. Heat olive oil in a large pot and add cumin seeds and chopped onion. Sauté. Add diced potatoes, carrots, peas, ginger/garlic masala, green chillie masala, thana jeeroo, red chillie powder, turmeric powder and 1½ teaspoons salt. Stir and cook, covered, on medium heat for 10 minutes, stirring occasionally.

3. Add half-cooked rice and spread evenly over vegetables. Add ½ cup water. Cover and cook on low heat for 15 to 20 minutes or until rice and vegetables are cooked.

4. Garnish with chopped cilantro and sesame seeds.

Ghee (Clarified Butter)

Ingredients:

1 pound salted or unsalted butter

Method:

1.   Place butter in a saucepan on low heat.
2.   Allow butter to melt and come to a rolling boil.
3.   Do not stir. Continue boiling for 15 to 20 minutes or until froth reduces considerably and you can see a clear gold liquid.*
4.   Remove pan from heat. Allow ghee to cool down.
5.   Strain ghee through thick layers of cheesecloth into a glass jar.
6.   Store ghee in a cool dry place.

*It is important for ghee to melt long enough to remove all milk solids. This will ensure that the ghee will not go rancid when stored in a cool dry place.

Condiments, Salads & Masalas

Tangy Tamarind Chutney
Cilantro Chutney
Apple Pickle
Fresh Tomato Chutney
Raita
Spicy Salsa
Zingy Carrot Salad
Katchoomber
Cucumber & Tomato Salad
Ginger/Garlic Masala
Green Chillie Masala
Garlic Masala
Garam Masala
Thana Jeeroo

Tangy Tamarind Chutney

Ingredients:

½ cup tamarind paste
1 cup water
1 cup ketchup
2 teaspoons garlic masala
2 teaspoons cumin, crushed
½ teaspoon red chillie powder
1 teaspoon turmeric powder
1½ teaspoons salt

Method:

1. Mix tamarind paste and water together in a bowl. Stir until paste is mixed in well.
2. Add ketchup, garlic masala, crushed cumin, red chillie powder, turmeric powder and salt. Mix well.
3. Store in refrigerator.

Cilantro Chutney

Ingredients:

3 bunches cilantro or 3 cups cilantro
2 green chillies (serrano or cayenne)
3 garlic cloves, peeled
3 teaspoons cumin seeds
½ teaspoon salt
juice of one lemon
1 teaspoon salt

Method:

1. Wash and drain cilantro in a colander.
2. Place cilantro, green chillies, garlic cloves, cumin seeds and salt in a chopper or food processor. Blend until chutney is a smooth paste.
3. Stir in lemon juice and 1 teaspoon salt just before serving.

Apple Pickle

Ingredients:

2 large Granny Smith apples
1½ teaspoons red chillie powder
1 teaspoon turmeric powder
2 teaspoons salt
1½ tablespoons olive oil

Method:

1. Peel and cut Granny Smith apples into chunks.
2. In a bowl, combine Granny Smith apples, red chillie powder, turmeric powder, salt and olive oil.
3. Mix well until spices coat all the apples.
4. Serve immediately.

Delicious with any vegetarian dishes in this cookbook, as a condiment.

Fresh Tomato Chutney

Ingredients:

1 large tomato, diced
1 tablespoon onion, finely chopped
2 tablespoons cilantro, finely chopped
2 tablespoons parsley, finely chopped
2 tablespoons green onions, finely chopped
1 teaspoon garlic masala
1 teaspoon cumin, crushed
¼ teaspoon red chillie powder
½ teaspoon turmeric powder
1 teaspoon salt
1½ teaspoons brown sugar
2 teaspoons white wine vinegar
1 tablespoon olive oil

Method:

1.   In a glass bowl, mix together tomato, onion, cilantro, parsley and green onions.
2.   Add garlic masala, crushed cumin, red chillie powder, turmeric powder, salt, brown sugar, white wine vinegar and olive oil.
3.   Stir well and serve immediately.

Raita

Ingredients:

1 cucumber, grated
¾ teaspoon salt
2 garlic cloves, grated
2 teaspoons cumin, crushed
¼ teaspoon red chillie powder
¼ teaspoon turmeric powder
¼ teaspoon mustard powder
4 tablespoons sour cream
1 cup plain yogurt

Method:

1.   Grate cucumber in a glass bowl and sprinkle with ¼ teaspoon salt and stir. Set aside in a cool place for 5 minutes.
2.   Squeeze grated cucumber with both hands to remove any excess water.
3.   Place squeezed cucumber in a separate bowl and add grated garlic, crushed cumin, red chillie powder, turmeric powder, mustard powder, ½ teaspoon salt, sour cream and plain yogurt.
4.   Mix thoroughly. Refrigerate raita before serving.

Spicy Salsa

Ingredients:

4 Roma tomatoes, diced
1 medium onion, chopped
1 cup cilantro, finely chopped
4 teaspoons thana jeeroo
3 teaspoons cumin, crushed
½ teaspoon red chillie powder
1 teaspoon salt
½ cup ketchup

Method:

1. In a bowl, combine diced Roma tomatoes, chopped onion, chopped cilantro, thana jeeroo, crushed cumin, red chillie powder and salt. Mix well.
2. Add ketchup and mix well.

Quick, easy and tasty!

Zingy Carrot Salad – page 97

Zingy Carrot Salad

Ingredients:

4 carrots, julienned
1 cup green onions, finely chopped
½ cup cilantro, chopped
2 tablespoons extra virgin olive oil
3 tablespoons cider vinegar
¾ teaspoon salt
¼ teaspoon red chillie powder
¼ teaspoon turmeric powder
1 teaspoon cumin, crushed
1 teaspoon brown sugar

Method:

1. In a bowl, place julienned carrots, finely chopped green onions and chopped cilantro.
2. In a small bowl, combine extra virgin olive oil, cider vinegar, salt, red chillie powder, turmeric powder, crushed cumin and brown sugar. Mix well to make a vinaigrette.
3. Add vinaigrette to carrot salad and toss just before serving.

Katchoomber

Ingredients:

½ English cucumber, julienned
½ small red onion, julienned
3 medium carrots, julienned
3 celery sticks, julienned
2 tablespoons cilantro, chopped
3 tablespoons extra virgin olive oil
2 tablespoons cider vinegar
¼ teaspoon red chillie powder
1 teaspoon cumin, crushed
2 teaspoons salt
1 tablespoon parmesan cheese, grated

Method:

1. Place julienned English cucumber, red onion, carrots and celery with chopped cilantro in a large salad dish.
2. Blend together in a small bowl, extra virgin olive oil, cider vinegar, red chillie powder, crushed cumin and salt, using a whisk.
3. Pour vinaigrette over salad and toss before serving. Garnish with grated parmesan cheese.

Cucumber & Tomato Salad

Ingredients:

1 English cucumber, cut in small cubes
2 Roma tomatoes, finely chopped
4 tablespoons cilantro, finely chopped
2 tablespoons green onions, chopped
1 teaspoon cumin, crushed
⅛ teaspoon red chillie powder
2 tablespoons olive oil
2 tablespoons cider vinegar
1 teaspoon salt
1 tablespoon toasted slivered almonds

Method:

1. Place cubed English cucumber, finely chopped Roma tomatoes and finely chopped cilantro in a salad bowl.
2. In a small bowl, combine finely chopped green onions, crushed cumin, red chillie powder, olive oil, cider vinegar and salt. Whisk until vinaigrette is blended.
3. Pour vinaigrette over cucumber and tomatoes. Toss before serving.
4. Garnish with toasted slivered almonds.

Ginger/Garlic Masala

Ingredients:

1 cup fresh garlic cloves, peeled
1 cup fresh ginger, peeled
3 fresh green chillies (serrano or cayenne)
¼ teaspoon coarse salt

Method:

1. Place garlic, ginger, green chillies and salt in a chopper or food processor. Blend until masala is a fine paste.
2. Fill small freezer bags with small amounts of ginger/garlic masala. Seal each bag and flatten so that the masala is about ⅛ inch thick. Store in the freezer.
3. When you require ginger/garlic masala, break off the amount you need and place the masala back in the freezer.

Ginger/Garlic Masala is used in most of the dishes in this cookbook.

Green Chillie Masala

Ingredients:

1 cup fresh green chillies (serrano or cayenne)
¼ teaspoon coarse salt

Method:

1. Wash and drain green chillies.
2. Place whole chillies and salt in a chopper or food processor. Process until masala looks like a paste.
3. Fill small freezer bags with small amounts of green chillie masala. Seal each bag and flatten so that the masala is about ⅛ inch thick. Store in the freezer.
4. When you require green chillie masala, break off the amount you need and place masala back in the freezer.

Green Chillie Masala is used in many of the dishes in this cookbook.

Garlic Masala

Ingredients:

1 cup fresh garlic cloves, peeled
2 fresh green chillies (serrano or cayenne)
¼ teaspoon coarse salt

Method:

1.   Blend garlic, whole chillies and salt in a chopper or food processor, until masala is a fine paste.
2.   Fill small freezer bags with small amounts of garlic masala. Seal each bag and flatten so that the masala is about ⅛ inch thick. Store in the freezer.
3.   When you require garlic masala, just break off the amount you need and place masala back in the freezer.

Garlic Masala is used in some of the recipes in this cookbook.

Garam Masala

Ingredients:

3 tablespoons coriander seeds
2 tablespoons cumin seeds
1 tablespoon black peppercorns
1 tablespoon whole cloves
¾ teaspoon cardamom seeds
1 tablespoons cinnamon sticks, broken into small pieces
1½ teaspoons star anise, in small pieces

Method:

1. Clean coriander seeds, cumin seeds, peppercorns, cloves and cardamom seeds by putting them through a small sieve to remove any dust, sand or sticks.
2. Place spices on a stainless steel tray and go through each of the spices to check for any large impurities, e.g. larger sticks, stones etc.
3. Using a mortar and pestle, break down cinnamon sticks and star anise into smaller pieces.
4. In a bowl, combine coriander seeds, cumin seeds, black peppercorns, cloves, cardamom seeds, cinnamon sticks and star anise. Mix well to make the garam masala blend.
5. In a coffee grinder*, add the amount of garam masala blend that the grinder can hold. Grind to a fine powder and place in a bowl. Continue until all the blend has been ground.
6. Allow garam masala to cool down. Stir well.

*The coffee grinder should be dedicated only to spices and not coffee. Store freshly ground spices in glass jars in a cool, dry place. Garam Masala will stay fresh for at least 1 to 2 years.

Tastfully Indian

Thana Jeeroo

Ingredients:

4 tablespoons coriander seeds
2 tablespoons cumin seeds

Method:

1.   Clean coriander seeds and cumin seeds by putting them through a small sieve to remove any dust, sand or sticks.
2.   Place spices on a stainless steel tray and go through each of the spices to check for any large impurities, e.g. larger sticks, stones etc.
3.   In a bowl, combine coriander seeds and cumin seeds. Mix well to make the thana jeeroo blend.
4.   In a coffee grinder*, add the amount of thana jeeroo blend that the grinder can hold. Grind to a fine powder and place in a bowl. Continue until all the blend has been ground.
5.   Allow thana jeeroo to cool down. Stir well.

*The coffee grinder should be dedicated only to spices and not coffee. Store freshly ground spices in glass jars in a cool dry place. Thana Jeeroo will stay fresh for at least 1 or 2 years.

Desserts

Cool Melon Dessert

Ingredients:

½ cantaloupe
½ honeydew melon
½ seedless watermelon
1 cup green seedless grapes
1 cup red seedless grapes
4 to 6 tablespoons honey
juice of half a lemon
4 tablespoons mint, finely chopped

Method:

1. Remove seeds from cantaloupe and honeydew melons.
2. Using a melon baller, scoop out balls of watermelon, cantaloupe and honeydew melons. Place in a large dessert bowl.
3. Add green and red grapes.
4. In a separate bowl, mix together honey, lemon juice and mint.
5. Pour mixture over fruit. Toss.
6. Cover and place in refrigerator. Serve cold.

Barfi

Ingredients:

1 cup ricotta cheese
2 cups skim milk powder
1 teaspoon cardamom, ground
1½ cups icing sugar
1 tablespoon pistachios, chopped

Method:

1. In a pot, place ricotta cheese, skim milk powder and ¾ teaspoon ground cardamom. Cook on low heat and stir.
2. Stir continuously for 15 to 20 minutes until mixture thickens.
3. Remove from stove and set aside. Allow mixture to cool until warm to the touch.
4. Add icing sugar and blend in well. Grease a 9-inch square pan and evenly spread barfi in pan. Cut into squares.
5. Garnish with chopped pistachios and remaining ground cardamom.
6. Allow barfi to cool. Remove squares from pan and store in an airtight container in the refrigerator.

Panda

Ingredients:

1 cup ricotta cheese
1 cup half-and-half cream
1¼ cup sweetened evaporated milk
2 teaspoons cardamom, ground
3 cups skim milk powder
1 cup icing sugar
2 tablespoons pistachios, chopped

Method:

1. In a pot, heat ricotta cheese, half-and-half cream, evaporated milk and 1½ teaspoons ground cardamom on low heat, stirring continuously.
2. Add skim milk powder a little at a time, while stirring, to avoid lumps.
3. Continue stirring for 40 to 55 minutes until mixture is thick.
4. Remove pot from stove and allow mixture to cool until it is warm to handle. Do not allow mixture to cool down completely as it will harden very quickly.
5. Add icing sugar and blend in well. Take small amounts of doughy mixture and roll into 1-inch balls, then flatten slightly to make a disc shape.
6. Garnish with chopped pistachios and remaining ground cardamom.

Store in a sealed container in the refrigerator.

Ladoo

Ingredients:

3 tablespoons ghee
½ cup chana flour
4 tablespoons almonds, ground
½ cup icing sugar
1 teaspoon cardamom, ground

Method:

1. Heat ghee in a saucepan on medium heat and add chana flour. Stir constantly for 5 to 10 minutes or until chana flour is lightly browned.
2. Add ground almonds and continue stirring for 3 to 5 minutes.
3. Remove pan from stove and add icing sugar and ground cardamom. Mix well.
4. Allow mixture to cool until warm to touch.
5. Form ladoos by making 1-inch balls with mixture.
6. Place ladoos on a plate and allow to cool. Store in refrigerator.

Serve cold. Makes approximately 10 ladoos.

Coconut Squares

Ingredients:

2 cups sugar
½ cup water
2½ cups unsweetened coconut, finely shredded
2 cups powdered milk
1 drop red food coloring
1 tablespoon unsweetened chocolate, melted

Method:

1. In a pot, heat sugar and water on medium heat, stirring regularly. Bring mixture to a rolling boil to make a syrup.
2. Remove syrup from stove and add unsweetened coconut and powdered milk. Mix well.
3. Divide mixture into 3 equal portions.
4. Line 9-inch cake pan with wax paper. Spread one portion of coconut mixture evenly in the pan.
5. Add red food coloring to one of the portions of coconut mixture to give it a pinkish color. Spread this portion of mixture evenly on top of the first layer.
6. Melt unsweetened chocolate in a double boiler on the stove or in a small bowl in the microwave. Add melted chocolate to the last portion of coconut mixture and blend.
7. Spread chocolate layer evenly over the pinkish layer.
8. Cut into 1-inch squares and allow coconut squares to cool for 2 hours.
9. Remove from pan carefully and place in sealed container. Store in refrigerator.

Mango Raas

Ingredients:

6 to 8 ripe mangoes, peeled and cut into chunks
½ teaspoon cumin, finely ground
¼ teaspoon white pepper, finely ground
¼ teaspoon dry ginger, finely ground

Method:

1.   Put mango chunks in a blender and blend to a smooth pulp. Sieve pulp through a plastic sieve.
2.   Add ground cumin, ground white pepper and ground ginger and stir well.

Traditionally enjoyed with Corn Roti (page 81), Spicy Potatoes (page 55) and Pakoras (page 17).

Mango Smoothie

Ingredients:

½ cup mango pulp
½ cup vanilla ice cream
1 cup milk
⅛ teaspoon ground ginger
5 ice cubes
mint leaves for garnish

Method:

1. In a blender, combine mango pulp, vanilla ice cream, milk, ground ginger and ice cubes.
2. Blend until smooth.
3. Pour into two 8-ounce glasses.
4. Garnish with mint leaves.

Notes

Meal Suggestions

Meal Suggestions

MEAL I	
Spicy Chicken Wings	18
Butter Chicken	35
Spicy Herb & Garlic Potatoes	24
Basmati Rice	84
Katchoomber	98
Cool Melon Dessert	107

MEAL II	
Chicken Tapeli	21
Lamb Vindaloo	39
Spicy Potatoes	55
Rotla (Millet Roti)	79
Cucumber & Tomato Salad	99
Coconut Squares	111

MEAL III	
Spicy Onion Rings	20
Jeera Salmon	46
Mixed Lentil Daal	66
Yellow Rice with Onions	86
Zingy Carrot Salad	97
Tangy Tamarind Chutney	91

Tastfully Indian

Meal Suggestions

MEAL IV

Barbecued Garlic Chicken Kebobs	37
Barbecued Spicy Lamb Chops	38
Spicy Herb & Garlic Potatoes	24
Cilantro Chutney	92
Katchoomber	98
Cool Melon Dessert	107

MEAL V

Onion Bhaji	27
Spicy Prawns	47
Spicy Potatoes	55
Corn Roti	81
Zingy Carrot Salad	97
Tangy Tamarind Chutney	91

MEAL VI

Papetas (Fried Eggplant)	25
Muttar Paneer	52
Corn Roti	81
Basmati Rice	84
Apple Pickle	93
Cucumber & Tomato Salad	99

Tastfully Indian

Meal Suggestions

MEAL VII

Patarya (Spicy Spinach Rolls)	26
Vegetable Korma	57
Chana Masala	53
Basmati Rice	84
Raita	95
Mango Smoothie	113

MEAL VIII

Dadima's Onion Soup	71
Sprouted Mung Bean Curry	65
Rotla (Millet Roti)	79
Basmati Rice	84
Raita	95
Barfi	108

MEAL IX

Chicken Tikka	34
Ground Beef Curry	43
Yellow Rice with Onions	86
Katchoomber	98
Cilantro Chutney	92
Cool Melon Dessert	107

Tastfully Indian

Meal Suggestions

MEAL X

Bataka Vadas	22
Spicy Lamb Roast	40
Spicy Herb & Garlic Potatoes	24
Tangy Tamarind Chutney	91
Cucumber & Tomato Salad	99
Mango Smoothie	113

MEAL XI

Pakoras	17
Indian-Style Cajun Chicken	36
Spicy Potatoes	55
Tangy Tamarind Chutney	91
Zingy Carrot Salad	97
Cool Melon Dessert	107

MEAL XII

Mango Raas	112
Corn Roti	81
Spicy Potatoes	55
Pakoras	17

Tastfully Indian

Glossary

Glossary

Ajwain seeds	carom seeds
Aloo	potatoes
Bake	to cook by dry heat inside an oven
Basmati rice	thin, long-grained rice with a delicate fragrance
Bataka	potatoes
Bhajyas	appetizers made with chana flour and chopped vegetables also known as Pakoras
Bhakro	baked savory dish made with rice and chana flour
Bind	to thicken liquids by the addition of thickening agents
Black mustard seed	used in many appetizers and vegetable dishes
Blend	mix ingredients together
Boil	cook food in large amounts of liquid until it bubbles
Butterflied	leg of lamb boned and cut part way through so the meat can be spread open to look like butterfly wings
Cardamom	green pods with aromatic black seeds
Cassia sticks	the outer bark of a cinnamon tree, used as a spice
Cayenne	hot red chillies, green when harvested early
Chai	tea
Chai masala	spice mixture to make spicy tea
Chana	chickpeas
Chana masala	chickpea curry with green peppers, onions and tomatoes
Chop	cut up in small pieces
Chutney	spicy condiment made with vegetables or fruit
Cilantro	herb grown from coriander seeds
Clarify	to remove impurities from a liquid or fat by heating, skimming and straining

Tastfully Indian

Glossary

Coriander	brown seeds used in making spice blends
Cumin	also known as jeeroo, commonly used in Indian dishes
Curry	a dish made with many spices
Daal	husked split beans
Dadima	grandmother
Deep-fry	cook by immersing in sufficient hot oil to cover food
Dice	cut into small cubes
Dokra	steamed lentil cake
Drizzle	pour liquid very slowly to gently cover food
Fillet	cut off piece of raw meat or fish removing skin and bones
Fry	to cook in small amount of fat in an open pan
Garam	warm
Garam masala	warm mixture – a blend of many spices
Garnish	decorate and flavor a dish with spices or herbs
Ghee	clarified butter
Gluten	proteins found in wheat grains, which are not soluble in water and which give wheat dough its elastic texture
Gobi	cauliflower
Grate	reduce food to small strips by rubbing on serrated surface
Half-and-half	a mixture of milk and cream that has 10% milk fat
Jeera	cumin
Jeeroo	cumin seeds
Julienned	vegetables cut in thin long strips

Glossary

Katchoomber	Indian salad
Knead	work dough by folding and stretching with heel of hand
Korma	curry made with coconut milk, ground almonds and yogurt
Ladoo	round sweet dessert
Mango raas	mango pulp
Marinate	soak food in seasoned liquid or paste to tenderize and flavor before cooking
Masala	mixture
Moothya	round patties shaped by hand and pan fried
Muttar	peas
Pakoras	deep-fried appetizers made with chana flour also known as bhajyas
Panda	sweet dessert made with sugar, milk and ricotta cheese
Paneer	mild milk curd cheese
Papetas	sliced fried eggplant with spices
Patarya	spicy spinach rolls
Pilaf	cooked rice with vegetables and/or meat
Poora	spicy crepes
Puri	crispy deep-fried bread
Raita	cucumber condiment
Raveya	stuffed eggplant
Red chillie powder	made from crushed hot red peppers
Roast	cook with little fat in an oven
Roti	unleavened flatbread

Tastfully Indian

Glossary

Rotla	bread made with millet flour
Sauté	cook food gently in a little fat in an open pan
Serrano	type of green chillie pepper
Sieve	pass liquid or dried food through a fine mesh to remove lumps
Steam	cook in steam from boiling liquid
Strain	to filter
Tamarind	tangy fruit used for making chutney
Tapeli	dish made with meat, onions and tomatoes with spices
Tawa	traditional Indian concave-shaped pan without an edge, made for cooking roti or naan bread
Thana	coriander seeds
Tikka	spicy skewers made of chicken, lamb or beef
Turmeric powder	bright yellow root, dried and ground
Urad	black mung beans
Urad daal	husked split urad beans
Vadas	fried crispy appetizers in the shape of little balls
Vindaloo	hot, spicy meat curry made with tomatoes, onions, and lime juice.
Vinaigrette	salad dressing made of vinegar, oil, herbs and spices
Whey	watery part of milk that separates from curds
Wok	deep pot with handle to fry or stir-fry food

Notes